To Sharon, something to rem

with all my love, always

Mike

x x

July 1988.

Victorian Lewes

Victorian Lewes

Compiled by

Colin Brent & William Rector

Phillimore

1980

Published by
PHILLIMORE & CO. LTD.
London and Chichester

Head Office: Shopwyke Hall,
Chichester, Sussex, England

ISBN 0 85033 355 5

Printed and bound in Great Britain by
BILLING & SONS LIMITED

List of Illustrations

TOWNSCAPE

High Street: St. Anne's

High Street: St. Michael's

High Street: School Hill

High Street: Eastgate and Cliffe

Panoramas

Southover High Street

COMMERCE

Transport

Acknowledgements

Our sincere thanks go to the following for permission to use photographs in their possession: Mr. L. S. Davey for numbers 20, 32, 34, 35, 58, 62, 69, 73, 95, 96, 100 and 107; the Commercial Square Bonfire Society for number 112; Mr. and Mrs. W. Rector for number 4, from J. T. Case, *Photographic Views of Lewes* (Baxter, Lewes, 1857); and the Sussex Archaeological Society for number 113 from the Bartlett Collection, numbers 42, 43, 57, 67, 77, 108, 109 and 114-121 from the Bedford Collection, and numbers 21 and 66.

The remaining ninety photographs have been copied from negatives in the Edward Reeves Collection, which is owned by *The Sunday Times* and administered by the Sussex Archaeological Society at Barbican House, Lewes. Our especial thanks are due to *The Sunday Times* for permission to use them: the royalties from this publication will be devoted to maintaining the Reeves Collection in a form which will allow the local historian more convenient access.

Our gratitude for help and information is also due to Miss Fiona Marsden, the Curator of the Archaeological Society's Museums, to Mrs. Joyce Crowe, Mrs. Bridget Giles and Mr. John Bleach, librarians at Barbican House, Lewes, to Mr. L. S. Davey and Mr. S. Hughes. The photographs have been prepared for publication by Mr. William Rector, Mr. Edward Reeves and Mr. Tom Reeves.

Introduction

Victorian Lewes was intensely alive. Its inhabitants were justly proud of their fine panoramas, medieval ruins and picturesque streets. But the place was no museum. The town was a busy centre of transport, exchange and manufacture, of the professions and local government. Religious life was dynamic and political passion often ran high. Lewesians, however, were not averse to recreation. Lectures, concerts, sports, circuses, fairs and the seaside were to hand.

Edward Reeves, a photographer of great technical skill and pictorial sensitivity, captured many facets of this fascinating town during a career in Lewes which lasted from 1854 until his death in 1905. His business at 159 High Street passed to his son and grandson, and should soon be resumed by his great-grandson, Tom. From the 1890s onwards a second photographer of flair and sensibility, Edward Bedford, was also recording the Lewes scene. Bedford went on to become Headmaster of Eastbourne College of Art and, after his retirement, Curator of the Lewes Borough Museum.

We have tried to do justice to the artistry of Edward Reeves and Edward Bedford, and to the vitality of the county town whose images they saved for posterity. William Rector has been responsible for the initial selection and Colin Brent for the commentary.

COLIN BRENT, M.A., D.Phil.
Brighton Polytechnic

WILLIAM RECTOR
formerly of the Museum of London

This volume
is dedicated to
Judith Brent
and
Zena Rector
in gratitude for
much help and
reinforcement

A photograph acquires something of the dignity which it ordinarily lacks when it ceases to be a reproduction of reality and shews us things that no longer exist.

The Baron de Charlus

Townscape

When Queen Victoria ascended the throne in 1837 Lewes had prospered for many decades as a commercial centre and a county town. Its nine thousand inhabitants were packed along or around a mile of High Street, which made a leisurely descent from the western downs into the floodplain of the river Ouse and across the bridge to the eastern suburb of the Cliffe. Beyond rose precipitous chalk, stretching away towards Mount Caburn. The sweeping panoramas of weald, brookland and downland, glimpsed from the street or surveyed from the castle, never failed to delight topographers. In 1724 Daniel Defoe had thought Lewes a 'fine pleasant town, well built, agreeably scituated in the middle of an open champaign country'. A hundred years later Thomas Horsfield, the county historian and a Unitarian minister at Westgate Chapel in Lewes, commented, 'Although on an elevated site, it is yet encircled by an amphitheatre of loftier hills, which give to it a truly picturesque and pleasant character'. William Morris was later to describe Lewes as 'set down better than any town I have seen in England'.

From the bridge across the Ouse radiated a web of road and river transport, which had long made Lewes a natural focus of marketing, manufacture and administration. The main avenue of commerce was inevitably the High Street, which contained over 140 shops and taverns, four hotels, the hop and corn exchange, and the markets for livestock and provisions. Bordering the High Street – around the castle precincts and the County Gaol to the north, down the sunny slopes to the south, and in the congested Cliffe – lay a network of courts, passages, twittens, back lanes and side streets, where spacious houses, some Elizabethan in origin, were often crammed close to slum tenements, workshops and pig sties. Also to the south, across the Winterbourne stream, strung out above the brookland, was the suburb of Southover, which had grown up at the gate of the Cluniac priory. Close to the banks of the river Ouse, north and south of the bridge, crowded industrial enterprises which depended on barge transport to and from Newhaven – gasworks, foundries, breweries, corn and seed warehouses, timberyards, a tanyard, a papermill, and wharves, for coal and for lime dug out from nearby chalk-pits.

During the solid prosperity of Georgian Lewes most earlier, timber-framed buildings had been fronted with decent wealden brick or mathematical tile, although patches of unregenerate weather-boarding and gable still evaded fanlight and cornice. By 1837 some substantial new town houses had also been erected, as well as a dignified residential terrace in Albion Street. A second was under construction at Priory Crescent in Southover. County Hall was the only swagger public building. The County Gaol brooded squatly in a back street. Being unincorporated, Lewes possessed no Town Hall, nor had its role as a social

Mecca for the local gentry created a permanent assembly room, theatre or promenade. Brighton had, perhaps, burgeoned too well and too near. The parish churches were in shabby decay, apart from All Saints, modishly rebuilt in 1806. Protestant Nonconformity was, architecturally, in better shape and could boast austere Temples of Dissent at Jireh and at Tabernacle. Recognising their town to be short on magnificence, Lewesians tended to dwell on their shattered medieval ruins, which evoked 'the true rust of the Barons' Wars'.

The Victorians did surprisingly little to transform the fabric of this Georgian townscape. The town's economy became mildly sluggish and its population grew with impressive slowness, from just over 9,500 in the 1840s to just under 11,500 in the 1890s. By the early 1870s some wealthy residents had removed to sombre Italianate villas on sunny slopes, mainly in St. Anne's Crescent and Rotten Row. Then came the many-gabled, tile-hung, turreted Wallands Estate, designed by men at least half in love with Norman Shaw. On the fringes of the town appeared a 'brickish skirt' of artisan terraces — along Western Road and South Street, around the railway station, and below Castle Green and St. John-sub-Castro.

Although few commercial facades in the High Street were remodelled, local industry was vital enough to cause the rebuilding of the waterworks, the Phoenix foundry, the gasworks, four breweries and the railway station (twice), while the all-conquering advance of the Principle of Utility brought a new County Prison, a Union Workhouse and two contiguous extra-mural cemeteries. But these buildings were erected on the fringes of the Georgian townscape. Even the railway lines which came to converge on Lewes occasioned only one bold visual intrusion, at the bottom of School Hill.

If economic and demographic growth proved sluggish, religious and cultural life increased steadily in vitality. Four new Nonconformist chapels, a Catholic church and several National Schools were erected, the British School was extended, and all seven parish churches were restored or rebuilt. The favoured style was a robust provincial Romanesque or Pointed, often with lavish use of local flint. The Fitzroy Memorial Library, the Freemasons' Hall and the School of Science and Art were the product of secular High Seriousness and came clad in academic High Gothic. In painful contrast was the hectic Italianate face of the new Town Hall, completed in 1893.

In this section the reader will be led down the High Street, across the bridge to the Cliffe, and then back along the southern slopes and through Southover. Many buildings, already mentioned, will be encountered in later sections.

HIGH STREET: ST. ANNE'S

1. The western approaches, *c*.1869. Joseph Shelley's mill and the County Prison crown the chalk ridge. From St. Anne's church the High Street descends past the castle to the river. Beyond the Cliffe the downs sweep up to Mount Caburn.

2. (*below*) St. Anne's parish, *c*.1869. The fields on the right stretching away from the Paddock were hallowed ground to Victorians. Across them in 1264 raged the battle which, 'greater in its consequences than Marathon or Waterloo', ensured 'the triumph of Constitutional Liberty'.

3. (*left*) Up St. Anne's Hill, *c.*1870. The chancel of St. Anne's church was given its Early English dressing in 1843. A dray delivers beer to *The Pelham Arms*, owned by the Southover brewer, William Verrall.

4. (*below left*) Down St. Anne's Hill in 1857. On the left stands the Shelleys, owned by Captain George D'Albiac, a descendent of the Shelley family. Opposite is the Ionic porch of Edward Monk, corn merchant and brewer at Bear Yard, a close friend of Richard Cobden. Past the gabled Grammar School, St. Anne's House closes the vista.

5. (*opposite above*) The Renaissance porch of the Shelleys, *c.*1865. The girl inside may be a daughter of the occupier, John Hodgkin, a Quaker barrister, who was already the father-in-law of the architect, Alfred Waterhouse, and of Edward Fry, later a Chancery judge.

6. (*opposite below*) The garden of the Shelleys. The mound and shell keep of the castle are picturesquely smothered by vegetation.

7. (*above*) St. Anne's House, *c.*1867. The High Street cork-screws towards Westgate past Rotten Row and Keere Street. St. Anne's House was occupied until 1867 by the boarding school of Mark Antony Lower, an essayist and historian. An earlier resident was the Jacobean antiquary, John Rowe.

HIGH STREET: ST. MICHAEL'S

8. Westgate from the east, *c.*1870. Above the excavated High Street, beyond *The Brewers Arms*, rises the gable of Bull House, once the home of Thomas Paine. Framed photographs hang in the window of Edward Reeves. Behind are St. Michael's church and the Town Clock.

9. Clock Cottage by St. Michael's church, *c.*1870. The unusual proportions of its facade contrast with the weather-boarded shopfront of William Banks, a confectioner, newsagent and supplier of C. T. Brock's fireworks.

10. The High Street under flags at Easter 1872. The Borough Decoration Committee has beflagged the High Street to welcome over ten thousand Volunteers marching out to manoeuvres on Newmarket Down.

11. Castle Place, 165-7 High Street, *c.*1870. This elegant composition, with distinctive ironwork and ammonite capitals, was built about 1810 by Amon Wilds and his son, Amon Henry. It housed the museum of the geologist, Gideon Mantell.

12. (*below*) The site of the livestock market, *c.*1870. A great-wheeled waggon manoeuvres outside *The White Hart Hotel*. The market for cattle, sheep and pigs took place each alternate Tuesday.

HIGH STREET: SCHOOL HILL

13. (*opposite above*) Towards County Hall, *c.*1870. The shopfront of Flint & Son, grocers, looks across to *The Star Hotel* and to the porch of George Whitfield, a partner in Lewes Old Bank.

14. (*opposite below*) Gentility and trade, 31-35 High Street, *c.*1870. Two fine private houses, Lewes House and School Hill House, are succeeded by the premises of Thomas Bance, tailor and woollen draper, and by the offices of *The Sussex Express.*

15. (*above*) Down School Hill, *c.*1870. The royal arms surmount the shop of John Hother, farmer, breechesmaker and woolstapler, who was for over thirty years Secretary of the Southdown Hunt. Across the Ouse, above the turning into Albion Street, broods the Rhenish helm of Undercliffe.

16. Albion Street, *c.* 1870. The long balconied terrace, built about 1830, exudes a select charm.

17. Up School Hill, *c.* 1870. Fashionable doctors and lawyers reside behind the stately elevations on the right.

HIGH STREET: EASTGATE AND CLIFFE

18. (*above*) Eastgate corner, *c.*1870. The High Street slips past the Lewes Dispensary and Infirmary and the Fitzroy Memorial Library to the railway arch, constructed and embellished in 1868. Beyond are the river bridge and Cliffe High Street.

19. (*right*) Lewes bridge before 1874. Its delicate span was designed in 1727 by Nicholas Dubois, the architect of Stanmer House, The corner of *The Bear Hotel* faces the shop of Samuel Solomon, watchmaker and silversmith.

20. (*opposite above*) Over the bridge in 1888. No other tree has punctuated the High Street since the descent of St. Anne's Hill. *The Bear Hotel* was a favoured resort of anglers and of the Brookside Hunt.

21. (*opposite below*) Along Cliffe High Street, *c.*1878. The two sides are architecturally contrasting. The cornices on the right reflect a comprehensive rebuilding in the late 1820s.

PANORAMAS

22. From Prospect Cottage, Chapel Hill, *c.*1890. Across the middleground the gasworks, the Morris iron foundry, the Bear Yard brewery, and corn and seed warehouses crowd the hidden banks of the Ouse.

23. (*opposite above*) From above the chalk-pit in Cliffe, *c*.1880. The railway curves between a coal wharf by the Ouse and the ornamental grounds of Leighside, the residence of Burwood Godlee, a Quaker corn merchant.

24. (*opposite below*) From St. Martin's Lane, *c*.1875. In the foreground stands Tanyard House with its sheds and vats. Between the Mount and the pavilion of the Dripping Pan is Mountfield House. Beyond, the Ouse winds through spreading brookland past Itford Hill towards the sea.

25. From Pipes Passage, *c*.1875. The view extends across Grange Road and Spring Gardens (Toby Town), past the breweries of William Verrall and Benjamin Morris, to Juggs Way snaking between the windmills on Cranedown.

SOUTHOVER HIGH STREET

26. (*left*) The bottom of Keere Street, *c.*1870. Legend asserts that George IV, when Prince of Wales, drove a coach and four down this steep descent to Southover Grange.

27. (*below left*) Southover Grange *c.*1865. Tradition maintains that the materials for this mansion were brought in 1572 from the dismantled Cluniac priory of St. Pancras.

28. (*right*) Priory Crescent, *c.*1870. The shed of Thomas Goldsmith, wheelwright and parish clerk, looks across from the manorial pound of Southover to the splendour of the Crescent. Ivy smothers the ruined Great Gate of the priory.

29. (*below right*) A happy blend of facades, *c.*1870. The posters in the window of Porched Houses on the left advertise the Horsham Fatstock Show.

30.   Porched Houses, *c.* 1870. This once desirable Tudor residence, popularly associated with Anne of Cleves, has degenerated into tenements for the labouring classes. The gas-lamps were not lit during a full moon.

Commerce

In 1837 Lewes was still a thriving centre of marketing and manufacture. A web of road and river transport focussed on its bridge, which commanded an important corridor between the weald and the Channel carved out by the river Ouse. The town was 'the centre of a great coaching district, comprising Brighton, Hastings, Eastbourne, Tunbridge Wells, East Grinstead, and many other places'. Its coaching inns, *The Star*, *The White Hart*, *The Crown* and *The Bear*, were busy and commodious. Lewes remained, too, a bustling port. In the 1790s the Ouse had been made navigable inland past Newick towards Lindfield, and the channel to Newhaven harbour had been improved. Locally based barges transported corn, seed, lime, chalk, timber, coal, iron and consumer goods to and from the wharves by the bridge, around which clustered gasworks, foundries, breweries, kilns, timberyards and warehouses.

Lewes continued to flourish in 1837 as a centre of exchange. Produce from downland, wealden and marshland farms was sold at the hop and corn exchange, at the livestock and provision markets, and at the annual wool and sheep fairs. The town's wholesale merchants also dealt in non-agricultural commodities — timber, lime, coal, groceries, wine and textiles. Customers from the surrounding countryside, who thronged the exchange, the markets and the fairs, also patronised the scores of self-employed butchers, bakers, grocers, chemists, drapers, tailors, milliners, cabinetmakers, saddlers, printers, builders, publicans and beer-shop-keepers, as well as a professional band of lawyers, doctors, portraitists, school proprietors and Dissenting ministers. Among those who had launched their careers in Lewes were Dr. Richard Russell, who popularised the drinking of sea-water in Brighton, Dr. Gideon Mantell, who uncovered the iguanadon, and Amon Wilds, who with his son, Amon Henry, built much of Regency Brighton.

Speculation on the rather sluggish economic and demographic growth of Lewes in the Victorian period must remain tentative. Some contemporaries blamed the advent of the railway system. Lewes quickly became an important junction. Lines were opened to Brighton and St. Leonards in 1846, to Keymer Junction and Newhaven Harbour in 1847, to Uckfield and Tunbridge Wells in 1858, and to East Grinstead in 1882. Yet local businessmen blamed rail transport for weakening the town's role as a distributive centre for groceries, ironmongery and other commodities, previously brought into Newhaven by sea. Others complained that rural customers now had rapid and convenient rail access to the ampler retailing resources of Brighton. The build-up of the railway network undoubtedly disrupted older forms of transport. Coaching quickly collapsed and in 1858 the last carrier between Lewes and London withdrew. Thereafter road haulage services radiated only as far as Nutley, Burwash and Hailsham. The railway also killed traffic on the Upper Ouse Navigation towards Lindfield. But barge fleets belonging to Lewes merchants still transported coal, timber, corn, seed and lime to or from Newhaven. Indeed in the 1870s, these merchants, Edward Chatfield, Robert Hillman, George and Samuel Elphick, Richard Rickman, George Newington, John Lucas and Caleb Kemp, were still the largest employers in Lewes. Apart from Chatfield, they also operated the chalk-pits at Southerham, Malling, Offham and Glynde.

From the mid-1870s the marketing and retailing life of Lewes was unavoidably damaged by the deepening agricultural depression which hit downland, wealden and marshland farming. Activity slackened at the corn exchange, the livestock market and the sheep fair. Rural customers grew fewer and poorer. There were frequent complaints that trade was 'dead'. In 1879 the livestock market was transferred from the High Street to a site by the railway station, a move which seems to symbolise the waning importance of agriculture.

But the local economic scene was not uniformly gloomy. Industrial activity remained buoyant. Seven breweries continued to flourish. Three generations of the Every family extended production at the Phoenix ironworks. Charles Wells, proprietor of the Fina foundry and Secretary of the Mechanics' Institute, was a resourceful technologist. *The Sussex Express*, founded in 1837 as a Conservative rival to *The Sussex Advertiser*, swiftly gained the largest circulation in south-east England. In 1859 Joseph Farncombe added a third successful newspaper, *The East Sussex News*. Under the direction of two cousins, Charles and John Latter Parsons, the stonemasons' yard at Eastgate built up a wide reputation. The building firm of Henry Card & Son designed and constructed such major jobs as Harveys brewery and the School of Science and Art (now Lewes Area Library). Such enterprises could often tap demand in the growing resorts of Eastbourne and Brighton. Local merchants and industrialists remained the backbone of the Newhaven Harbour and Ouse Lower Navigation Company, the Lewes Waterworks Company, and the Lewes Gas Light and Coke Company. Many were also prominent railway promoters in the 1840s and 1850s.

In this section the reader will examine road, river and rail transport, the sheep fair, retailing, the drink trade, industrial enterprise and public utilities.

TRANSPORT

31. (*top*) A coach and four outside *The Star Hotel*, *c.* 1888. A coach service between Eastbourne and Brighton operated in the summer season until the mid-1890s. Horses were changed at *The Star*.

32. James Urry, coal dealer and furniture remover, *c.* 1900.

33. The port of Lewes, *c.*1868. A barge is moored behind the footbridge which connects the foundry and the warehouse of the Etna ironworks, owned until 1868 by Henry Attwood Thompson. To the right are corn and seed warehouses, to the left *The Bear Hotel.*

34. (*opposite above*) The gasworks, *c.*1870. A barge unloads coal for the Lewes Gas Light and Coke Company. Behind lay the iron foundry of Ebenezer Morris, senior deacon of Jireh chapel, and Chairman of the Poor Law Guardians.

35. (*opposite below*) On the Ouse Lower Navigation, *c.*1890. Below the downs west of Mount Caburn a river barge plies between Lewes and Newhaven Harbour.

36. (*above left*) The first railway terminal. This handsome station in Friars Walk was completed in August 1846 by the London, Brighton and South Coast Railway Company to serve the recently opened Brighton to St. Leonards line. Trains ran in and out which required complex manoeuvring.

37. (*left*) The new railway station, *c.* 1867. 'The building is in the Gothic style, and its architectural features have a very pleasing effect'. However questionable may be this contemporary verdict, the new station, opened in November 1857, was much more conveniently sited.

38. (*above right*) The new station: the London line, *c.* 1867. The venerable gentleman in the tall hat is the station master, James Brook.

39. (*above*) The new station: the Brighton line, *c*. 1867.

40. A locomotive tragedy in September 1879. At 3.16 p.m. on Saturday, 27 September, Engine No. 174, standing at the London platform, exploded with a sound 'not unlike the discharge of an immense piece of ordnance'. The driver was killed and several railwaymen were scalded.

41. (*opposite above*) The September sheep fair, *c*. 1870. In the late 1860s between forty and fifty thousand Southdowns might be penned. Bob Copper in *A Song For Every Season* remarks that such fairs were 'as firmly embedded in the minds of the sheepfarming fraternity as the religious feasts and fasts are in the thoughts of a church congregation'.

42. (*opposite below*) Southdowns at the fair in 1891. The breed was world famous for its wool, succulent meat, hardiness and low feed costs.

43. A shepherd at the fair in 1891.

RETAILING

44. A confectioner and news-agent at 157 High Street, c. 1867. William Banks, a local historian and member of St. Michael's Burial Board, opened the first newsagency at Lewes in 1857.

45. A poulterer and fishmonger at 53 High Street, c. 1875. George Coppard was a staunch Conservative, like his neighbour James Pelling, the bootmaker. To the left of his Christmas birds are the seasonable cards of Arthur Morris, postmaster and stationer.

46.   A grocer and cheesemonger at 3 North Street, *c*.1878. Beneath the mathematical tiles are the frontage of Henry
Baker, baker, Cornelius Harris, house agent, and Gilbert Jenner.

47. (*right*) Pope's Passage between 178 and 179 High Street. The passage separates *The Rainbow Tavern* from the premises of Henry Curtis, chemist, druggist and mineral water manufacturer.

48. A draper and general outfitter at 214 High Street, *c.*1880. The Unitarian, William Crosskey, placed the firm of Browne and Crosskey in 'the front rank of county trade'. Of his four Liberal sons, William became spiritual adviser to Joseph Chamberlain, Robert a County Magistrate for Sussex, Rowland mayor of Lichfield, and Walter second mayor of Lewes. Beyond the chestnut stands the crisp facade of Eastgate stoneworks.

49. (*above*) Newcastle House at 181-3 High Street, *c.*1872. Leased in 1734 to the Duke of Newcastle as a political club and coffee house, its frontage is here divided between a plumber, painter and glazier, a saddler and basketmaker, and a branch of the London and County Bank. At No. 180 hangs the bun of George Corner, tobacconist and clay pipe manufacturer.

50. (*left*) Neighbours to the new Freemasons' Hall at 151-3 High Street, *c.*1869. Beside its High Gothic diapering and finely twisted drainpipes stand the premises of Joseph Ransom, hairdresser, David Wall, shoemaker and exciseman, and George Corner, soon to move to No. 181.

51. (*above*) A saddler and harnessmaker at 31 North Street, *c.*1870. The shopfront of Josiah Weller abuts the yard of George Harman, builder, carpenter, joiner, surveyor, house agent, furnishing undertaker and insurance agent.

52. (*left*) The London and County Bank at 59 High Street, *c.*1885, showing the recent late Perpendicular facade.

THE DRINK TRADE

53. *The Star Hotel, c.*1875. Robert Geer, who owned *The Star*, was also proprietor of the adjacent corn and hop exchange. The potted plants of Albion Russell, boot manufacturer and amateur florist, bloom above leggings and galoshes. In 1874 his daughter married G. F. Bromley.

54. *The White Hart Hotel, c.*1868. Its facade faces the loggia of County Hall. To the left a hanging top-boot, advertising the products of William Gates, and to the right *The Unicorn,* a beershop owned by Harvey's brewery.

55. (*above*) *The Crown Hotel* at 191 High Street, *c.*1875. Next door rises the tower of the provision market, built in 1792

56. (*opposite above*) *The Swan* in Southover High Street, *c.*1870. A milkboy leans between *The Swan,* owned by the brewer, William Verrall, and the scorched front of a blacksmith's forge. Samuel Hillman, who shoed nearby, was in turn Headborough, Constable and Ale-conner of Southover.

57. (*opposite below*) Verrall's brewery in Southover High Street, *c.*1900. Behind the house on the corner lay a second brewery, developed by W. S. Morris and rebuilt about 1878 by Ballard & Company.

58. Lyell's Steam Brewery at North Street, South Malling, in 1887. The brewery looms above *The Brewery Tap*, formerly *The Tanners Arms*. The tanyard lay across the road. Next door stands *The Wheatsheaf*, owned by Beard's brewery.

INDUSTRY AND PUBLIC UTILITIES

59. George Baxter (1804-1867). Baxter became celebrated as a pioneer of the printing of finished coloured drawings. His father, John, originator of the inking roller, established himself as a bookseller and printer at Lewes in 1802. His brother, William, built up *The Sussex Express,* and his nephew, Wynne, became first mayor of Lewes.

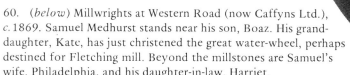

60. (*below*) Millwrights at Western Road (now Caffyns Ltd.), *c.*1869. Samuel Medhurst stands near his son, Boaz. His grand-daughter, Kate, has just christened the great water-wheel, perhaps destined for Fletching mill. Beyond the millstones are Samuel's wife, Philadelphia, and his daughter-in-law, Harriet.

61. (*above left*) Riverside industry, *c.*1870. The railway to Uckfield cuts across the timberyards and sawmills bordering the Ouse. By Greenwall are the Phoenix ironworks, owned by the Every family, who proved model Unitarian employers.

62. (*far left*) A brig at Higham's Wharf off South Street. Some think this ship to be the coal brig, *Halifax*, undergoing repairs in 1839. Others identify it as *The Eagle*, built at the Lewes shipyard of Edward Chatfield. His yard launched *The Richard and Emily* in 1862 and *The Wallands* in 1866.

63. (*above*) An extension to the waterworks in 1869. Workmen tidy up after the installation of a 60-horse pumping engine by Messrs. Easton, Amos & Anderson. To their right stands a daring Mannerist portal.

64. (*left*) The new gasometer in 1869. Labourers employed by Messrs. Pigott & Son pause from constructing a new gasholder by the Ouse for the Lewes Gas Light & Coke Company at a cost of £5,910 10s.

65. The road up outside 74-75 High Street, *c.* 1875. Labourers and bystanders are grouped outside the premises of Joseph Shelley, baker and miller, the Unitarian manager of the St. Michael's soup kitchen.

Church and State

The Reform Act of 1832 confirmed Lewes as a Parliamentary Borough, returning two members, but extended the constituency to include Southover and the Cliffe. Apart from the Poor Law Union, this was the only administrative link between the 'old Borough' and its two suburbs until municipal incorporation in 1881. Whigs and Tories each secured a parliamentary seat in 1841. But in 1845 local Conservatives bitterly divided over the Corn Laws and concessions to Irish Catholics. Their member, Henry Fitzroy, remained loyal to Sir Robert Peel and formed an alliance with local Whigs which kept the Borough non-Tory until 1874. Lewes Liberalism also benefited from the vitality of Protestant Nonconformity and from the support of the Lord Lieutenant, the third Earl of Chichester, whose heir, Lord Pelham, was M.P. from 1865 to 1874. The constituency was merged in 1885 into a new Mid-Sussex division which remained strongly Conservative.

Until municipal incorporation in 1881 Lewes was a palimpsest of autonomous jurisdictions. An annual Court Leet chose two High Constables for the 'old Borough', who conducted parliamentary elections, received proclamations, despatched loyal addresses, summoned Town Meetings and supervised certain properties, amenities and trusts. The Cliffe and Southover had separate Courts Leet. Responsibility for lighting, paving and cleansing the streets lay with a body of Improvement Commissioners, who satisfied a property qualification, but again the two suburbs had their own authorities. The 'old Borough' and the Cliffe also maintained separate Volunteer Fire Brigades. In 1854 St. Michael's parish set up a Burial Board to establish an extra-mural cemetery: in 1873 the parishes of All Saints and the Cliffe set up their own Board to run another cemetery next to it. Although all seven parishes had been obliged in the mid-1830s to form a Poor Law Union, only in 1868 was a central Workhouse erected.

Lewes was also a county town. The assizes and the quarter and intermediate sessions for East Sussex were held. These judicial and administrative functions brought employment to local lawyers and a touch of pageantry to the High Street. The town also housed a growing number of felons, whose meagre diet was supplied by local tradesmen. The County Prison, rebuilt on a new site in 1850-3, was extended in 1869 to accommodate more criminals from a booming Brighton. The old Gaol in North Street, after receiving Crimean prisoners of war, marines and invalid convicts, became a Naval Prison in 1862. The Sussex Artillery Militia maintained its regimental depot by the Newhaven Road at Southover from its formation in 1853 until 1883. Its recruits, largely drawn from 'the agricultural population', were billetted for a few weeks at a time, largely in licensed premises. In 1859 the Lewes bourgeoisie, especially its Tory-Anglican members, rallied to form a Rifle Club, which became the 4th Sussex Rifle Volunteers.

After a great Volunteer review on the nearby downs at Easter in 1872, some tradesmen hoped that Lewes might become a major military centre. Local boarding school proprietresses were not amused.

Religious life in Lewes grew intenser during the Victorian period. From the mid-1860s the Church of England renewed its strength. Its seven incumbents became fully resident and ever eager in good works. Its churches were extended, remodelled and cleared of private pews. Sunday School classrooms were provided. The Central National School, built in 1840, was supplemented after the Education Act of 1870 by Voluntary Parochial Schools. These averted the indignity of an elected School Board. The government of the endowed Grammar School was overhauled. The theological tone of Lewes Anglicanism was 'Protestant'. Its anti-Catholic sentiment was shared by local Conservatism and by the Bonfire Societies. Both appealed to anti-Irish, anti-Popish and anti-Puseyite feeling. Successive rectors at St. Michael's who flirted with Ritualism were sonorously denounced on 'the Fifth'. In 1871 mobbing occurred after the opening of the Catholic church.

Protestant Nonconformity in Lewes was a powerful, if fissiparous force. Vigorous congregations existed of Independents (Tabernacle), Baptists (Eastgate), Presbyterians (Hamilton), Quakers, Wesleyan Methodists and Unitarians (Westgate). All but the last co-operated closely in evangelical and Sunday School activity. With the Unitarians they formed the backbone of local Liberalism and of its cultural focus, the Mechanics' Institute. But one influential sect stood apart. The High Calvinist congregation at Jireh, with 410 Sunday School scholars in 1887, was strongly Conservative and anti-Catholic in temper and cherished close links with 'Bonfire'. But even the High Calvinists united with other Dissenters to fund the British School, which was extended in 1863. In addition three Dissenting academies were available in the 1860s, run by William Button and Daniel Griffiths, both Baptists, and by John Dudeney, the Methodist son of the 'Shepherd Schoolmaster'.

A common focus of charitable action was the Lewes Dispensary and Infirmary, established in 1847. Besides the usual parochial charities, a number of private welfare organisations operated. The Lewes Town Mission promoted 'the moral and religious interests of the poorer classes, by visits to the sick and dying, services in Cottages and Workhouse, and the distribution of tracts'. A group of Quakeresses ran the Lewes Girls' Home to prepare 'Friendless Children' for domestic service. The Maternal Society provided 'clothing, coals and nourishment for respectable married women during their confinement'.

In this section the reader will encounter the activities of the Borough, Union and Parish, the County Town, the Military, the Church of England and Protestant Nonconformity.

BOROUGH, UNION
AND PARISH

66. (*above*) A Borough parliamentary election in April 1859. The High Constables, accompanied by the Town Crier, are ranged on the hustings before County Hall to declare the result. The Peelite, Henry Fitzroy, and the Whig, Henry Brand of Glynde Place, a future speaker, handsomely defeated two Conservatives, who were strong 'Protestants'. Gladstone became Chancellor of the Exchequer for a second term.

67. A parliamentary election in July 1892. The sitting Conservative member for Mid-Sussex, Sir Henry Fletcher, arrives for the declaration at County Hall. The balcony of *The White Hart* is loaded with blooms from The Primrose League. Sir Henry polled 5,621 votes and his Liberal opponent 2,322. Gladstone became Prime Minister for a fourth time.

68. (*left*) The Town Crier. Charles Wood, master cow-keeper, poses with his bell, badge and stave against a bucolic backdrop. For 37 years until 1881 he attended the High Constables. Besides calling the hour and the weather, he summoned 'pretty maids' to prepare the festive board on Christmas Eve.

69. (*below*) A Corporation procession in 1885. Destined for St. John-sub-Castro, they debouch into Commercial Square. The Mayor, Alderman Thorne, a retired China tea merchant, is preceded by the Mace Bearer and flanked by the Town Clerk. Behind is Alderman Caleb Kemp, a Quaker lime merchant.

70. (*opposite*) The Golden Jubilee celebrations on 21 June 1887. Between *The White Hart* and County Hall are brigaded 2,500 school children. They participate in a service of thanksgiving, conducted by the Reverend Perfect of St. John-sub-Castro, and assisted by the Volunteer and Town Band.

71. (*above left*) Lewes Union Workhouse. This model institution 'entirely separates the several classes of inmates 123 of whom it is adapted to receive'. The inmates could be visited on Wednesdays. The infirmary lies to the left.

72. (*left*) The extra-mural cemeteries c.1880. They contain a double demarcation. The farther serves St. Michael's parish, the nearer All Saints and the Cliffe. Each has a separate Burial Board. Within each are two mortuary chapels, one for Anglicans, the other for Nonconformists.

73. (*above right*) A devoted gravedigger. Mrs. Edward Steere plies a spade at the cemeteries. Her husband was sexton of St. Michael's. After his death in 1879 she carried on his work 'No mother prepares her baby's first bed with greater care and conscience'.

74. (*right*) The Cliffe Volunteer Fire Brigade, c.1870. The Captain, Benjamin Thorpe (with the epaulettes) the Lieutenant, the Engineer and sixteen men parade with their engine. Thorpe, a Baptist builder, commanded the Brigade for 21 years.

75. County Hall, *c.* 1885. Built in 1808-12 of Portland stone, its facade carries Coade reliefs depicting Wisdom, Justice and Mercy.

76. (*below*) The majesty of the Law, *c.* 1882. The carriage, attendants and trumpeters of the assize judges stand opposite St. Michael's church.

77. The majesty of the Law again, April 1892. Now the trumpets are sounding at the top of Station Street.

78. (*above*) The County Prison. Built in 1850-3 for £56,000, the harsh flintwork, dark Romanesque portal, heavy machicolation and naked cell gratings have an unmistakable message for the baker's boy. The residences of the Governor and the Chaplain flank the entrance.

79. (*left*) The Russian memorial. This fine obelisk, carved by John Strong, a Lewes mason, stands in the churchyard of St. John-sub-Castro. 'Raised by order of His Majesty the Emperor of Russia, Alexander II, 1877', the obelisk commemorates Finnish prisoners captured during the Crimean War, who died in the old County Gaol in North Street.

80. (*opposite above*) Officers of the Sussex Artillery Militia, *c.*1875. They brave the camera near their regimental depot in Southover. Behind them are massive limbers for the carriage of stores.

81. (*opposite below*) A Militia serenade, *c.*1865. The flags of Empire wave over an improvised bandstand amid the ruins of the Cluniac priory of St. Pancras.

82. (*above*) The cream of the Volunteers in 1871. The N.C.O.s of the 4th Sussex Rifle Volunteers (Lewes) muster in the castle keep. Not subject to military law, they could resign after due notice.

83. The apotheosis of the Volunteers on Easter Monday in 1872. From beneath this triumphal arch, designed by the Town Surveyor, Frank Davey, over ten thousand Volunteers marched forth along the Brighton Road to do battle on Newmarket Down. 'The flags overhead, the diversified uniforms, the crashing of bands.. the galloping of field officers were quite exhilarating'. Over 200 large flags and many tons of laurel, holly, acuba, lauristinus and yew adorned their route.

84. St. John-sub-Castro, *c.*1870. Rebuilt in 1839 to accommodate a fast growing parish, the church looks across Gallows Bank to Paddock Lane and Hangman's Acre.

85. (*above left*) The interior of All Saints church before 1883.
The pulpit, the Tablets of the Law and a massive Italian painting
of the Baptist in prison loom down on a galleried preaching-box,
built in 1806 by Amon Wilds and his son, Amon Henry.

86. (*left*) The interior of St. Michael's church after 1878. Within
the new chancel ritualism is rife.

87. (*above*) St. Michael's congregation on Ascension Day in 1881.
Headed by Mrs. Cross, the rector's wife, 27 lady fund-raisers pre-
pare to lay commemorative stones in the wall of the new Sunday
School and Parish Room, on the site of Clock Cottage. In the High
Street some less regenerate gather to spectate.

88. (*above*) The Sunday School Centenary Festival in July 1880. Sunday School scholars from five Anglican parishes gather in Manor Field at Southover, by permission of William Verrall, for tea, bread and butter, swings, foot races, kiss-in-the-ring and scrambling for sweets.

89. The Central National School, *c*.1885. Two stone Charity Children in Georgian dress gesture from its neo-Tudor facade built in 1840.

90. The Tabernacle Chapel (Independent). This striking neo- Grecian Temple of Dissent, enlarged in 1832, is flanked by the ironmongery of Charles Aspull Wells, a local pioneer of electric light, who succeeded Henry Attwood Thompson as proprietor of the Etna ironworks in 1868.

91. (right) The interior of the Tabernacle. The pulpit rises from the deacons' enclosure to dominate a gracefully unified auditorium. In 1868 the wealthy congregation included the builder, Henry Card, the stonemasons, Charles and John Latter Parsons, the ironfounder, Henry Attwood Thompson, and the brewer, William Harvey.

92. (*opposite*) The Wesleyan Chapel in Station Street, *c*.1875. The Methodists disperse from their Chapel, built in 1867. The Sunday School below was completed in 1874.

93. (*right*) The Quaker Meeting House, *c*.1870. This modest structure, built in 1784 next to the churchyard of All Saints, belies the wealth and vigour of its small congregation, many of whom were members of the Rickman family or related to it.

94. (*below*) A Quaker boarding school, *c*.1873. The daughters of Quaker farmers and 'charming Irish girls, who came to rub off their brogue', gather in the garden of 65 High Street. The school was conducted by three spinsters, Rachel Special and Mary and Catherine Trusted, 'utterly conscientious and kindly teachers . . . dressed in the primmest, neatest, plain gowns, and muslin or net caps'. Among the scholars, probably, is Maude Robinson, authoress of *A South Down Farm In the Sixties*.

95. The Rotunda of the British School in Lancaster Street, c.1898. William Sweatman, a local shopkeeper, stands outside this derelict octagon, built in 1809 to allow a central master to supervise the instruction given by monitors, a pedagogic device associated with Joseph Lancaster. The School, once the pride of Lewes Nonconformity, was closed in January 1897.

Recreation

During the Victorian period recreation grew more complex and, often, more organised. The cultivation of the mind made strenuous local advances. The discovery at the priory by railway navvies of the bones of its founders, William and Gundreda de Warenne, led in 1846 to the formation of the Sussex Archaeological Society, which maintained a museum in the barbican of the castle. In 1862 the volumes of the Lewes Library Society were sumptuously rehoused in the Fitzroy Memorial Library (a gift too majestic to be maintained by a more recent generation). The town's professional elite formed a Monday Evening Club to hear papers on the execution of Charles I, the legal system of Jersey and the World before the Deluge. From 1868 the School of Science and Art held 'day classes for ladies and separately for gentlemen, and evening classes for artisans and general students'. Until the late 1870s the reading room, library, lectures and entertainments at the Mechanics' Institute in West Street offered a focus for popular self-improvement. Thereafter, these facilities were dispersed more widely, among Temperance and Co-operative Societies and the clubs attached to Church and Chapel. Music was made by visiting performers, Harmonic and Choral Societies and the Militia and Town Band.

In 1837 the only organised sports in or near Lewes were the matches of the Bowling Green Society and the Priory Cricket Club, the race meetings held in the summer, and the meets of the Southdown and Brookside Hunts. After 1859 the 4th Sussex Rifle Volunteers staged annual shooting matches and athletic sports. In 1860 Swimming Baths were built by public subscription. A Bicycling Club and a Rowing Club were added in the 1870s. The next two decades saw organised sport steadily widen.

Traditional unorganised recreations lingered on — skating at Falmer and Beechwood ponds in winter, marbles, quoits and sledging at the Coombe on Good Friday, garlands and Jack-in-the-Green on May Day, foot races near Newmarket Hill, boating on the Ouse and at the Pells, the September sheep fair, public executions and their pallid substitute, watching for the black flag to be run up. One ancient spectacle, 'Bonfire', went from strength to strength. After rioting in the 1840s its future seemed in doubt, but the restoration of a territorial Catholic hierarchy to England gave renewed strength to anti-Popery and greater sanction to 'the Fifth'. From the 1870s imperialist and xenophobic sentiments mingled with older 'Protestant' prejudice. The boundaries of innocent pleasure enlarged. Visiting circuses grew more various and glittering. The railway excursion ticket allowed families, Sunday School scholars and Friendly Society members to picnic in hospitable parkland at Glynde Place, Stanmer and Conyborough and to taste the delights of Eastbourne and Brighton.

96. (*left*) The barbican of the castle in 1896. Its facade proclaims the fiftieth anniversary of the Sussex Archaeological Society, whose museum of antiquities was housed above the gateway.

97. Antiquities within the castle keep, *c.*1870. The medley on display includes a dugout canoe, a cannon from Newhaven harbour, stocks and a whipping post, alabaster figures of Hercules and Minerva from Herstmonceux Castle, and the Castle Warder.

98. The Fitzroy Memorial Library before 1868. Designed in 1862 by Sir Giles Gilbert Scott and built at the expense of Henry Fitzroy's widow, a daughter of Baron Nathan Rothschild, the Library supplies a Ruskinian touch to Eastgate. On its shelves were eight thousand volumes of standard English works owned by the Lewes Library Society.

99.   A Chess Club, *c.* 1890. Mental sensibility radiates from the group. Lewes Chess Club was refounded in 1886.

100. (*above*) Lewes Horticultural Society Show, *c*.1890. The fruits and blossoms, the product of much thoughtful care, are marshalled in the Corn Exchange.

101. The British Workmen's Institute in Little East Street. Built in 1871 at the expense of a Quakeress, Elizabeth Payne, its reading and refreshment rooms offer to mechanics 'the social advantages and comforts of a public house, without the temptation to indulge in intoxicating drinks'. Its lecture room gave an early platform to Joseph Arch and other apostles of Agricultural Unionism.

COMPETITIVE SPORTS

102. The Lewes Bowling Green Society, c.1880. Matches had been played on the green within the castle bailey since the early seventeenth century. Along the front row, from left to right, are Thomas Monk, brewer at Bear Yard, Dr. J. G. Braden, George Newington, corn and lime merchant, Robert Crosskey, draper and cement manufacturer, John Head, chemist, John Verrall, landowner, Richard Lambe, upholsterer, an unknown member, John Lucas, a partner of Newington, James Broad, candle manufacturer, and Harvey Ellman, farmer. Along the back row stand Dr. Frank Hall, Dr. Ticehurst, John Hampton, practical brewer at Bear Yard, H. W. Wolff, editor of *The Sussex Advertiser,* the Reverend S. W. Thomas, Colonel H. F. Mackay, Chief Constable of East Sussex, and John Maxfield Smith, owner of Harveys brewery.

103. (*opposite above*) A local cricket eleven, c.1865. They are probably members of the Priory Club which was formalised in 1831. The seated batsman in the foreground with his elbow on the table is H. M. Hyndman, who later became an influential, if erratic exponent of Karl Marx. He played for Sussex in 1864 and during a match at the Dripping Pan in September 1865 against the United South of England XI he scored nine runs and took three catches for the Priory Club.

104. (*opposite below*) Ladies for cricket, c.1880. A reticent gentleman makes up the eleven.

105. Ladies at croquet, *c.*1866. They are manoeuvring on the bowling green in the castle precincts.

106. (*opposite above*) A local Bicycle Club, *c.*1875. Dismissed in reactionary circles as 'Cads on Casters', they parade with their machines on the bowling green.

107. (*opposite below*) Roller skating at 140 High Street, *c.*1878. The rink adjoins the Lewes and County Club, which also provided rooms for reading, smoking, dining, cards and billiards. In 1876 rinking was 'the newest and most popular pastime of the present time', but it was not long in vogue.

108. (*above*) Lewes races on 7 August 1891. They are under starter's orders for the Astley Stakes, won by Mr. N. Fenwick's Gossoon. Several training stables were established in the town.

109. (*above right*) Lewes races on 8 August 1891. The Saturday crowd is favoured with fine weather. There were hopes in the 1860s that Lewes might become a second Epsom.

110. (*right*) Edward VII at Lewes races, *c.*1905. The King-Emperor has diverted his attention from the ladies.

111.   'The Fifth' in the High Street, *c.*1876. The crowds watch the culmination of 'Bonfire'. The Pope and Guy Fawkes are consumed by fire between County Hall and *The White Hart*. Masked revellers frisk in the street. The artist of the oil painting is unknown.

112.   Commercial Square Bonfire Society in November 1879. To the left of the seated Archbishop of St. John-sub-Castro stands the Commander-in-Chief clad as a British general, and to the right the First Lieutenant in a clown's suit. The current Zulu and Afghan wars account for the recumbent King Cetewayo with assegai and for the two Mahratta princes in silver chain armour.

113. 'The Popish Pedlar' in November 1913. Stalwart Protestants from the Cliffe Bonfire Society admire this 'gigantic figure of a monk holding in one hand a rosary and a tray of ornaments in the other'. The effigy was accompanied in the procession on the Fifth by a model Bleriot monoplane, with aviator. Ragtime music was provided on a whistle pipe and a one string violin.

114.   Lord George Ginnett's circus on 24 July 1891. The elephants belonging to this 'old established equestrian troupe' lumber past the Fitzroy Library at midday. They drew large crowds.

115.   Lord John Sanger's circus on 13 August 1891. The imposing procession of this 'gigantic equestrian establish-
ment' descends St. Anne's Hill in the early afternoon.

116. (*above*) The
September sheep fair,
c. 1891. Ladies examine
a stall of household
accessories.

117. The same fair.
A cheap-jack beguiles
his audience.

118. The same fair. C. & J. Harris's steam merry-go-round attracts the children.

119. An excursion to Eastbourne in August 1892. Children ignore the apple seller to gaze at Punch and Judy. Behind stretches the monumental Grand Parade, built in 1851-5.

120. The same excursion. Refreshment is taken near the pier.

121. The same excursion. A rowing boat is launched onto a placid ocean.

122.   A group photographed, *c.* 1870. They are gathered round a viewer against a drawing-room backcloth in the garden of Edward Reeves.